Super Science!

Reader's Theatre Scripts and Extended Activities for the Primary Classroom

Written and Developed by Lisa Blau

Copyright © 1994
One From the Heart
Educational Resources

All Rights Reserved
Printed in the United States of America
Published by One From the Heart Educational Resources
14150 NE 20th Street • Suite #223
Bellevue, WA 98007

ISBN 0-9640333-3-X

This book is dedicated
to teachers everywhere
who recognize that as
educators we can inspire
our students to read, to write,
and most importantly, to
dream. I applaud all of you.

Table of Contents

♥ Introduction 6

♥ Helpful Hints 8

♥ Rocks, Rocks, Rocks! Let's Learn About Geology 13

♥ Our Spectacular Solar System 25

♥ What's it Like to be a Geologist? 41

♥ Radical Reptiles 47

♥ Water Wise - All About Water Conservation 63

♥ Feathered Friends..79

♥ Volcanos 97

♥ Dazzling Dinosaurs 107

♥ Reading Certificates 119

Daniel

Super Science!

Dear Readers,

Welcome to the wonderful world of science! In this exciting resource book you'll discover countless strategies for creating a literature-based science program that you and your students will <u>love</u>! The Reader's Theatre scripts and extended activities featured in this book support current research which emphasizes the effectiveness of the interdisciplinary approach. You will find ready to reproduce activity pages, booklists, and masks. There are easy recipes and art projects to try with your students. And in an effort to engage families in the learning experience, there are several "Family Fun Super Science Experiments" which feature easy hands-on experiments for students and their families to try at home.

Get ready to watch your students soar as they experience these exciting scripts and extended activities.

Happy Reading!
Lisa Blau

Be on Top of It All...
R•E•A•D!!!

♥ One final note...many of the illustrations in this book were made by my students. I am indeed proud of their help in making this book become a reality.

Helpful Hints

♥ As a speaking, listening, reading, and writing experience, Reader's Theatre will make a unique contribution to your curriculum. Your students will gain confidence in their oral reading as they perform the scripts. There are also countless opportunities for students to heighten their ability to listen when engaged in the Reader's Theatre experience. Student interest in the subject matter being performed is just one more piece of evidence to support the use of Reader's Theatre in the classroom. Finally, Reader's Theatre is great fun, and because of this, your students will be drawn into the learning experience. Come on, give it a try!

♥ If you have not used Reader's Theatre with your students, I would suggest using one of the shorter scripts such as, "Dazzling Dinosaurs." Be sure to model what I call, "Reader's Theatre Etiquette" with your students. Students must speak in a loud, clear voice and use lots of expression and enthusiasm while reading. Students must also hold the scripts in front of themselves at chest level so that their faces are not buried deep behind the scripts.

♥ Highlight each speaker's part on one set of scripts and then randomly pass a class set of scripts out to all of your students. Those students receiving a highlighted copy will be the first to perform the script. Once the script has been read, the members of the listening audience can trade scripts with a student who has just finished reading. Herein lies the beauty of using Reader's Theatre, <u>everyone</u> in the class has a chance to be a reader and a listener. In other words, all of your students will be actively engaged in the reading process.

♥ As educators we know the value of modeling for our students. To be truly successful with Reader's Theatre, make sure that you sit at the students' desks and model proper audience behavior and that you also read one of the parts thereby demonstrating how to read with enthusiasm and inflection. Be that positive, nurturing force to inspire the students in your class to achieve great things!

♥ Any of your favorite pre-reading activities can be employed when using Reader's Theatre. One easy tip for a vocabulary lesson is to ask students to mark any new or unfamiliar words on their scripts. These words can be listed on the board and discussed. Students could keep a log of science terms based upon the vocabulary found in the scripts.

♥ One highly effective teaching strategy is to use the graphic organizer known as a Knowledge Chart. Prior to reading a script, ask students to share what they know about the script's subject matter. As students supply information, write their comments onto a chart under the heading marked, "Prior Knowledge". After the script has been performed, students can return to the chart and tell about new facts that they have learned. This information is listed under the heading, "New Knowledge."

♥ A sample of a Knowledge Chart and a reproducible student copy can be found on pages 11 and 12. I suggest that you employ the use of the Knowledge Chart whenever you share the scripts with your students. It is a highly effective way to engage all students in the learning experience.

♥ To enhance your students' self-esteem, and to help you evaluate student participation, simply write the student's initials after each comment on your Knowledge Chart. The little gestures that you employ truly help your students feel proud of themselves and what they are learning.

KNOWLEDGE CHART

Name: **Kelli**   Subject: **Solar System**

Prior Knowledge	New Knowledge
(1.) There are 9 planets.	(1) Jupiter has 16 moons
(2.) Mercury is closest to the sun.	(2.) Saturn has 18 moons.
(3.) Pluto is the farthest from the sun.	(3.) The earth is 93 million miles from the sun.
(4.) The earth is about the same size as Venus.	(4.) Jupiter is the biggest planet.
	(5.) Mars is called the red planet
	(6.) Saturn has rings around it.

KNOWLEDGE CHART

Name: | Subject:

Prior Knowledge	New Knowledge

Rocks! Rocks! Rocks!

Let's Learn About Geology

A Super Science Script
Written and Developed by Lisa Blau

Narrator #1
Narrator #2
Basalt
Sandstone
Mr. Rockhound

Geologist #1
Geologist #2
Quartz
Miss Rockhound

Granite
Shale
Limestone
Slate

Narrator #1 -   Good morning! Welcome to our program called . . .

All -   ROCKS! ROCKS! ROCKS!

Narrator #2 -   Today you will learn all about rocks.

Geologist #1-   I am a geologist. I study rocks so that I can learn more about the earth. Afterall, the earth is made up of many kinds of rock.

Geologist #2 - I am a geologist too. Rock is the hard, solid part of the earth. Rock lies beneath the oceans and under the polar ice caps.

Narrator #1 - Rocks and minerals are useful to us in many ways. Take a look around your house and city, you will see rocks used in many helpful ways.

Narrator #2 -

Maybe you have a brick fireplace in your house. Maybe you have a garden wall made of stones. Your driveway and street are made from cement. Cement is made from crushed rocks.

Mr. Rockhound - Hello, my name is Mr. Rockhound. I enjoy collecting all different kinds of rocks.

Miss Rockhound -

I am Miss Rockhound. I like to collect rocks and minerals too. I can trade them with my friends. Collecting rocks is fun because we can learn so much about our earth by looking at rocks.

Geologist #2 -   Miss Rockhound is right! There are three main kinds of rocks. Each kind of rock tells us how our earth was formed.

Basalt -   The three main types of rocks are igneous, sedimentary, and metamorphic.

Mr. Rockhound -   Take a look at this piece of basalt in my collection. It is an igneous rock.

Geologist #1 -   Right you are, Rocky! Igneous rock was formed from magma deep within the earth. Igneous rocks form when magma cools and becomes solid.

Basalt -    My name is Basalt. I am a type of igneous rock. I can be dark green, gray or black in color. I am the most common of all rocks.

Granite -    Hello! My name is Granite. I am a type of igneous rock too. I was once liquid magma deep within the earth. I am gray with black and white crystals.

Quartz - Hello! I am a piece of quartz. Quartz is a type of igneous rock. I am <u>very</u> hard. I rank #7 on the hardness scale. Quartz can be clear or milky white.

Geologist #3 - We geologists have found lots of granite in the mountains in North America.

Granite - Many people use granite to build statues and buildings. I am strong and tough. The next time you pass by a statue or monument, take a closer look. That statue may be made from me, Granite!

Miss Rockhound - The second type of rock is called sedimentary rock.

Geologist #2 - Sedimentary rock was formed in layers. Sedimentary rock is made when minerals, plants, and fossils compress together.

Shale -  Hello! I am a piece of shale. I am the most common type of sedimentary rock. I was formed from many, many layers of mud.

Limestone -  Good morning! I'm a piece of limestone. Limestone is a kind of sedimentary rock, too. Limestone is used mostly for making buildings.

Shale - Shale is used for making bricks and cement. Shale is made up of quartz and minerals found in clay.

Limestone - Limestone is used for building and for making chalk.

Sandstone -  Good morning, rockhounds! I'm a piece of sandstone. Sandstone is another type of sedimentary rock.

Slate - Hello! I am a piece of Slate. Slate is a type of metamorphic rock.

Geologist #2 - Metamorphic rock can be formed by hot magma or by pressure and heat. It can also be formed as the earth's crust moves.

Slate - Soft shale and clay harden together to form slate.

Geologist #1 - Marble and quartzite are two other kinds of metamorphic rock.

Slate -	People use slate to make chalkboards. Slate is also used for making buildings. It is perfect for roofing because it is weatherproof and long-lasting.
Mr. Rockhound -	Wow! We have learned a lot about rocks today. Maybe you would like to collect rocks like me.
Miss Rockhound -	Collecting rocks is fun and interesting. You can learn how to identify rocks by using some of the information that you learned here today.
Mr. Rockhound -	You can also see many interesting rocks at a museum. You will be able to see all kinds of rocks, minerals, and fossils.
Geologist #2 -	And who knows . . . maybe you'll like learning about rocks so much that you'll go to college and study to become a geologist just like me.
Geologist #1 -	Or me!
Narrator #2 -	See you later, rockhounds!
All -	The End!

- Make a list of words that appear in the script that may be unfamiliar to your students. Read and discuss the list. This pre-reading activity will enable students to gain a greater understanding of the script's content.

- Have several different groups of students perform the script thereby allowing for all students to participate as a reader and as a member of the listening audience. Encourage students to listen for key information. You may even list these ideas on the board:

Listen and Learn:

- What are the three main types of rock?
- How do people use rock?
- What does quartz look like?
- What is limestone used for ?

- Employ the use of a graphic organizer known as a Semantic Analysis Chart. After reading through the script several times, ask students to supply the information for each square on the chart. Is someone uncertain about a fact or two?!!! No problem!!! Students will need to read the script again to find the missing information. The Semantic Analysis Chart can be completed by the entire class or it can be completed by a group of students. An individual student copy ready to reproduce and use with your students can be found in this unit.

- One of the benefits of using Reader's Theatre is that it can be used as part of an exciting lesson with your upper grade buddies. Have your primary grade students perform the script for their upper grade buddies. Your students may also wish to share their Semantic Analysis Charts with their buddies at this time.

- As a follow-up buddy activity, place the following items on a large tray:

  - a piece of aluminum foil
  - a metal spoon
  - a soda pop can
  - a lead pencil
  - a pair of scissors
  - a hand mirror
  - a piece of chalk

Show the tray and its contents to the students for thirty seconds, then cover up quickly. Upper grade students will help their primary grade partners fill in the, "Buddy Geoscavenge" page found in this unit. This activity calls for visual memory and some cooperative problem solving! The first pair to successfully complete the page wins a prize...a bookmark, or course. You'll find two reproducible bookmarks in this unit.

- Upper grade buddies can also help your students complete the activity entitled, "Geo-Pals Data Sheet." You'll need to set out the following rock samples for your students to refer to while completing the activity together:

  - basalt
  - sandstone
  - granite
  - quartz
  - slate
  - gneiss

Buddy Geoscavenge

Read the clues below to determine the names of the mineral products below.

1.   I'm something that is used to cover leftover food.

    _____

2.   Your teacher uses me when she writes on the board.

    _____

3.   You'll need me if you want to eat a dish of ice cream.

    _____

4.   Peek-A-Boo! I see you! People use this item to see their reflection.

    _____

5.   Hey! Cut it out! People use this item to cut paper.

    _____

6.   I store a refreshing drink.

    _____

ROLKHOUND

7.   You are using one right now to write down all the answers to the Geoscavenge.

    _____

*   **Buddy Challenge** - Write three clues for other everyday items made from minerals and share them with your friends!

Geo-Pals
Data Sheet

A I am a kind of igneous rock. I am dark in color. I am the most common of all igneous rocks. _____	**B** I am soft and grainy. If you rub with your fingers, some sand will come off in your hand. _____
C I am a kind of igneous rock. I'm very hard. I rank #7 on the hardness scale. I can be clear or milky white. _____	**D** People use me to make chalkboards. I am a kind of metamorphic rock. _____
E I am an igneous rock. I was once magma. I am usually gray with white crystals. _____	**F** I am made by heat and pressure. I was once a piece of gray granite. Now I am dark and my crystals are separated into layers. _____

This Geo-Pals Data Sheet was completed by Partner #1 _____ and Partner #2 _____

Learning About Geology is really cool!

Rocks! Rocks! Rocks!
A Semantic Analysis Chart

Type	How is it formed?	Kinds	Uses
Igneous Rock			
Sedimentary Rock			
Metamorphic Rock			

Geology Bookmarks

Copy back-to-back for 2-sided bookmarks

If you'd like to learn more about geology, don't miss these <u>SUPER</u> books

- <u>Rocks and Minerals</u>
  The Eyewitness Books Series
  by Dr. R.F. Symes

- <u>Rocks and Soil</u>
  by Terry Jennings

- <u>The Science Project Book of the Earth</u>
  by Steve Parker

- <u>Hands-On-Science</u>
  Earthquakes to Volcanoes
  by John Clark

Make a list of all the books that you have read about rocks and the earth:

_____

_____

_____

_____

* Once you've filled in this page, show it to your teacher for a neat treat!

I

Really

D-I-G

Books!!!◆

by Mike H.

I

Really

D-I-G

Books!!!◆

by Brittany

Our Spectacular Solar System

A Super Science Script
Written and Developed by Lisa Blau

Star Gazer #1
Star Gazer #2
Star Gazer #3

Star Gazer #4
Star Gazer #5

Star Gazer #5 - Welcome to our presentation called...

All - Our Spectacular Solar System.

Star Gazer #1 - Did you know that there are nine planets in our solar system? The planets all rotate around the sun. Let's find out about them right now.

Star Gazer #3 - Mercury is the planet that is closest to the sun. It is <u>very</u> hot on Mercury. The temperature can be as high as 800°!

Star Gazer #5 - Boy, you'd better be sure to wear your sunglasses on Mercury!

Star Gazer #2 -   Mercury is covered with craters.
                   There are no plants or animals on
                   Mercury.

Star Gazer #1 -   Venus is the second planet closest
                   to the sun. Venus is called the
   Earth's twin because these two
                   planets are almost the same size.

Star Gazer #5 -   Venus is sometimes called the
                   "morning star" and the "evening star"
                   because we can see Venus most
                   easily at these times.

Star Gazer #3 -   Venus is covered with very thick
                   yellow clouds. It is hotter on Venus
                   than on Mercury because these
                   clouds keep the heat from escaping.

Star Gazer #4 -   The Earth is the middle planet. Four
                   planets are bigger than the Earth
                   and four planets are smaller than the
                   Earth. The Earth has one moon.

Star Gazer #2 -   The Earth is 93 million miles from
                   the sun. If the Earth were closer to
                   the sun, it would be too hot for
                   plants, people, and animals to live
                   on it.

Star Gazer #1 -   If the Earth were farther from the sun, it would be too cold for plants, people and animals to live on it.

Star Gazer #5 -   It takes the Earth 365 days to go around the sun. We call this one year.

Star Gazer #2 -   Mars is the fourth planet from the sun. Scientists have named Mars the "Red Planet" because it looks red when we see it at night.

Star Gazer #3 -    Mars is very dusty and has craters and mountains. Its surface is very rocky. Mars has two small moons.

Star Gazer #4 -   Gee, I always thought that Mars was just a tasty candy bar!

Star Gazer #1 -   Jupiter is the fifth planet. Jupiter is the biggest planet in our solar system.

Star Gazer #5 -   Jupiter is so big that if it were a hollow ball, 1,000 Earths could fit inside of it!

Star Gazer #3 -   Wow! That's amazing! What else can you tell us about this super planet?

Star Gazer #4 -   Jupiter is covered with brown, yellow and reddish clouds.

Star Gazer #2 -   Jupiter has 16 moons. Jupiter is very far from the sun. It is <u>very</u> cold on Jupiter.

Star Gazer #5 -   Saturn is the sixth planet. Saturn is the second largest planet. Saturn has rings around it. The rings are made of tiny bits of ice and dust.

Star Gazer #1 -   Saturn has eighteen moons. Saturn is 886 million miles from the sun.

Star Gazer #4 -   Uranus is the third largest planet. Uranus is the only planet that rotates on its side. Scientists do not know why this happens.

Star Gazer #2 -   Uranus has 15 moons. It also has at least eleven rings. It takes Uranus 84 earth years to go around the sun.

Star Gazer #5 - Wow! You'd sure have a long time between birthdays!

Star Gazer #4 - Neptune is the fourth largest planet in our solar system. Neptune has four rings and eight moons.

Star Gazer #1 - Neptune is bright blue. Strong winds blow on the planet Neptune. These winds blow around the planet in the opposite direction of its spin.

Star Gazer #3 - Wow! It must be tricky to fly a kite on Neptune!

Star Gazer #2 - Pluto is not only the smallest planet in our solar system, it is also the farthest planet from the sun.

Star Gazer #1 - Scientists discovered the planet Pluto in 1930. Pluto is covered with frozen methane gas. Pluto is pinkish - brown in color. It is so far away from the sun, that it is dark and <u>very</u> cold.

Star Gazer #3 - Wow! And I always thought that Pluto was Mickey Mouse's dog!

Star Gazer #5 -   Well, super star gazers, we have really learned a lot about our spectacular solar system.

Star Gazer #4 -   If you'd like to learn more about our solar system, just head right down to the library and check out a few good books.

Star Gazer #3 -   My favorite book about the solar system is called <u>Journey to the Planets</u> by Patricia Lauber.

Star Gazer #5 -   And I enjoyed reading <u>Planets, Moons, and Meteors</u> by John Gustafson.

Star Gazer #1 -   If you like funny books you'll love <u>Dogs in Space</u> by Nancy Coffelt.

Star Gazer #2 -   Arf! Arf! Woof! Woof! It's wonderful!

Star Gazer #5 -   Have a great day and thanks for being a great audience.

All -   The End.

- Create a Semantic Analysis Chart for students to record information about each of the nine planets. After reading through the script with alternating groups of readers, students can add information to the chart. I like using Semantic Analysis Charts because they help children organize information in an ordered and easy to understand format. With 60% of our students favoring the visual modality, the Semantic Analysis Chart can be a powerful strategy to use with our students. Best of all, it can be adapted to use with any area of the curriculum! You can create a large-sized Semantic Analysis Chart for your students, or you can have students create individual charts. Cooperative grouping is also an option for this <u>extremely</u> effective teaching method. A reproducible chart is included in this unit for individual student responses.

- Encourage students to find out more information about the solar system to add to the Semantic Analysis Chart. Be sure to leave some of the headings blank on the Semantic Analysis Chart. Now you can challenge your students to come up with their own ideas for headings! My students added a column about the number of rings or moons each planet may have and a column about NASA exploration to each planet. Challenge students to create their own columns - they'll learn more if they are more actively engaged in the learning process! (Note: You will notice that there is a blank section on the reproducible page for this very purpose.)

- Encourage students to do some of their own star gazing! Check to see if your local community college offers family star viewing nights or field trips to their planetarium. <u>Science and Children Magazine</u> features a monthly stargazer's guide which can be reproduced and sent home for students. Write or call for information regarding this outstanding resource: <u>Science and Children Magazine</u> Publication Sales, National Science Teachers Association, 1742 Connecticut Ave. NW, Washington, DC 20009-1171 (202) 328-5800.

- How are craters formed?! This easy hands-on experiment will help students understand how craters are formed on the surface of the moon and the planets of our solar system. Spread a thin layer of flour onto a cookie sheet. Have students drop rocks onto the flour and watch the results. Have students try using larger and heavier rocks and try dropping the rocks from a greater distance. Instruct students to record the results of this experiment into their science journals.

- Read! Read! Read! Here are a few <u>great</u> chapter books to share with students during your solar system unit of study:

  - <u>Let Me Off This Spaceship!</u>
    by Gery Greer and Bob Ruddick
    Harper Trophy Books, 1991.

  - <u>Jason and the Aliens Down the Street</u>
    by Gery Greer and Bob Ruddick
    Harper Trophy Books, 1990.

  - <u>Aliens for Breakfast</u>
    by Jonathan Etra and Stephanie Spinner
    Random House, 1991.

  - <u>Aliens for Lunch</u>
    by Jonathan Etra and Stephanie Spinner
    Random House, 1992.

- Read! Read! Read Some More! You won't want to miss <u>Dogs in Space</u> by Nancy Coffelt, one of the books mentioned in the script. It's a delightful book with many extensions. Coffelt provides information about Planet 10. Use the reproducible page provided in this unit for students to write about what life may be like on Planet 10. In addition, students could also write about the continuing adventures of the dogs in space, or for added fun, students could write about any number of animals exploring space including dinosaurs, gorillas, or their pet hamsters! This book is full of possibilities!

- Write! Write! Write! Author Nancy Coffelt is one author who will write a fabulous letter to your students. I so enjoy having my students write to favorite authors as it is a way to show children that there is a purpose for writing. Remember what noted educator Lucy Calkins tells us about children and writing, "Educators <u>must</u> create writing assignments that are meaningful, relevant, and personal in order to truly motivate their students." So reach for the stars...write to author Nancy Coffelt!

> Nancy Coffelt
> c/o Harcourt Brace and Company
> 525 B Street
> San Diego, CA 92101

- Coffelt's brilliant artwork can provide your students with ideas for their own planetary creations. The "Artfully Quick and Easy" activity provided in this unit will truly add to your students' enjoyment of your solar system unit.

- Don't miss Loreen Leedy's superb book, <u>Postcards From Pluto</u>. This clever book is also **FULL** of countless extensions for students. The book's format, postcards being written home to family and friends by children exploring space, can provide the perfect springboard for your students. Use the accompanying worksheet for students to write their own, "Postcards from Pluto".

SOLAR SYSTEM
SEMANTIC ANALYSIS CHART

PLANET	DISTANCE FROM SUN	SIZE	NUMBER OF MOONS	ADDITIONAL FABULOUS FACTS		
Mercury						
Venus						
Earth						
Mars						
Jupiter						
Saturn						
Uranus						
Neptune						
Pluto						

Dogs in Space

by Nancy Coffelt

Create super illustrations to go with this favorite book by trying one of these activities:

* Make drawings with crayons of favorite animals drifting through the solar system...don't forget the space helmets! Press hard, then color over your picture with a black crayon. Use the side of a coin to scratch off the black crayon...your animals in space will look just like the ones in the book!

* What does Planet 10 look like? Create your very own planet using oil pastels on black paper...it will look REALLY cool!

The Mysterious Planet 10

Many scientists believe that there may be another planet beyond the orbit of Pluto. Imagine that you are an astronomer and that you have just discovered the Mysterious Planet 10. Write a science journal page that tells about your amazing discovery.

I have named the new planet _____
because _____.

The planet has these unique features _____
_____
_____

People on earth will be amazed to learn that on this new planet _____
_____
_____

* <u>To All Awesome Astronomers:</u>

Be sure to draw pictures of your planet and the aliens who live on your planet on the back of this page.

Cooks in the Classroom

Stars and Moon Cheese Toast

Here's a fun recipe to try after learning about the solar system! It's OUT OF THIS WORLD!!!

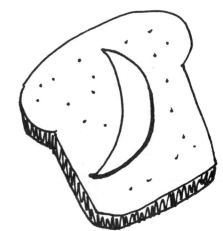

Here's What You'll Need

- 2 loaves whole wheat bread
- 2 packages American Processed cheese
- 1 tub soft margarine
- plastic knives
- toaster oven

Here's What You Do:

- Spread margarine on two slices of bread

- Use the plastic knife to cut star and crescent moon shapes from two slices of cheese

- Place the cut out shapes onto the bread and toast until bubbly...YUM!

Postcards From Pluto

by Loreen Leedy

Greetings from _____

TO:

Directions for Earthlings: Imagine that you have traveled to your favorite planet. Describe your adventures by writing a postcard to someone special! Design an illustration that shows where you have been on the other side of this card. Be sure to add lots of fabulous facts!

Super Star Gazer's Booklist

*   <u>Dogs in Space</u>
    by Nancy Coffelt

*   <u>Planets, Moons and Meteors</u>
    by John Gustafson

*   <u>Journey to the Planets</u>
    by Patricia Lauber

*   <u>Where Are the Stars During the Day? A Book About Stars</u>
    by Melvin and Gilda Berge

*   <u>Saturn</u>
    by Seymour Simon

*   <u>Jupiter</u>
    by Seymour Simon

*   <u>Star Gazers</u>
    by Gail Gibbons

*   <u>Sun Up, Sun Down</u>
    by Gail Gibbons

*   <u>A Book of Planets for You</u>
    by Franklin Branley

*   <u>The Sun is Our Nearest Star</u>
    by Franklin Branley

*   <u>The Magic School Bus - Lost in the Solar System</u>
    by Joanna Cole

*   <u>Postcards from Pluto</u>
    by Loreen Leedy

What's it Like to Be a Geologist?

A Super Science Script
Written and Developed by Lisa Blau

Student #1
Student #2
Student #3

Geologist #1
Geologist #2
Geologist #3

Student #1 -   Good morning! Welcome to our presentation of, "What's it Like to Be a Geologist?"

Student #2 -   To tell you the truth, I don't even know what a geologist is!!

Student #3 -   Well, if you've ever wondered where rocks come from or what our earth is made of, then a geologist could help you.

Student #1 -   That's because geologists study the earth and what the earth is made of.

Student #3 -   And that's not all...geologists do many other things. Some geologists look for oil and precious metals.

Student #1 -   Some geologists look for water deep within the earth.

Student #3 -   Some geologists study fossils. They look for dinosaur bones that tell us what life was like millions of years ago.

Student #2 -   Wow! Geologists sure are busy! It sounds like they do all kinds of neat stuff! I think I want to be a geologist when I grow up! Tell me more!

Student #1 -   Well, let's have some geologists tell you all about their work.

Geologist #1 -   I study earthquakes and volcanos. I travel to faraway places to learn more about the earth. Someday soon we geologists hope to learn how to predict earthquakes.

Geologist #2 - I use a seismograph to measure earthquakes. Geologists are trying hard to learn how to predict earthquakes so that we can help protect people and property.

Geologist #3 - I travel the world in search of petroleum. People need gas for our cars and oil to heat our homes. My job is a hard one because petroleum is not easy to find. Sometimes geologists find petroleum under the ocean.

Student #2 - What does it take to become a geologist?

Geologist #1 - Well, first you will have to go to college and study math, chemistry, and other important subjects.

Geologist #2 - It takes many years of study and hard work.

Geologist #3 - Once you become a geologist, you may go to faraway places or make a new discovery that can help people all over the world.

Student #2 -   Gee, if I become a geologist, I might even discover my own dinosaur! WOW!

Student #3 -   Wow! That would be great!

Student #1 -   And you can name it after me!

All -   The End

Evasaurus

- Make a list of words from the script that describe a geologist's work and tools. This list may include:

fossil   petroleum   volcano

dinosaur   earthquake   seismograph

- Ask students to try to define each word. It would be helpful to have photographs or drawings to help students gain a better understanding of the contents of the script. The visuals also make for greater interest in this exciting unit of study.

- There are many excellent books for children about geologists and their work. A visit to your public library can prove to be a wonderful source for materials to add to this unit of study. Don't forget to look for children's science magazines featuring articles about geologists and the earth.

- Two of my favorite books to share with my students are:

  - The Science Project Book of the Earth
    by Steve Parker
    Marshall Cavendish Corporation

  - The Hands-On-Science Book of Earthquakes To Volcanos
    by John Clark
    Gloucester Press

Reading is RADICAL!

Radical Reptiles

A Super Science Script
Written and Developed by Lisa Blau

Zoologist #1	Turtle	Snake
Zoologist #2	Gila Monster	Tuatara
Zoologist #3	Crocodile	

Zoologist #1 - Good morning! We're here to tell you about a very special group of animals.

Zoologist #2 - These animals have dry, scaly skin. They are cold-blooded. These animals can be found all over the world except in Antarctica.

Zoologist #3 - Some live in the tropical rain forests. Some live in the desert. Others live in the ocean.

Zoologist #1 - Can you guess what kind of animals we are talking about?!!

Zoologist #2 - These animals are . . .

All - Radical Reptiles!

Zoologist #3 - Some people are afraid of reptiles. They think that all reptiles are harmful. Crocodiles may attack and kill people and the Gila monster and several kinds of snakes are poisonous, but most types of reptiles are harmless. In many parts of the world people eat reptile meat and reptile eggs. Some reptiles are hunted for their skin. Reptile skin can be made into boots, belts, and shoes.

Zoologist #1 - Zoologists have divided reptiles into four main groups.

Gila monster - Lizards and snakes.

Turtle - Turtles.

Crocodile - Crocodilians.

Tuatara - Tuataras.

Zoologist #3 - What are tuataras?

I'm a radical reptile!

Beth

Tuatara - Well, allow me to introduce myself . . . I am a tuatara. Tuataras live off the coast of New Zealand. We look like lizards but we are more closely related to dinosaurs.

Zoologist #1 -   Our friend the tuatara is right! Dinosaurs that roamed the earth millions of years ago were reptiles.

Tuatara -   Tuataras have scaly, gray or greenish skin and are about two feet in length. We sleep during the day in our underground homes. Tuataras hunt at night.

Zoologist #3 -   What do tuataras eat?

Tuatara -   We eat insects, snails, birds, and frogs. We have very sharp teeth.

Zoologist #1 -   Please tell us more.

Tuatara -   If an enemy is chasing us and catches us by the tail, we have an easy way to escape. Tuataras can shed their tails! But that's no problem, because we can always grow a new one.

Zoologist #3 -   I'd like to learn more about some other reptiles.

Turtle -   Hello there! I am a turtle. Turtles are the
                  only reptiles with shells. There are about
                  250 different kinds of turtles. You can find
                  us in deserts, forests, rivers, ponds, and
                  oceans.

Zoologist #3 -   Please tell us more!

Turtle -   Turtles come in all kinds of sizes, colors,
                  and shapes. The largest turtle is the
                  leatherback turtle. Leatherbacks can be 8
                  feet long! The box turtle is only 4 inches
                  long!

Zoologist #3 -   Most turtles can pull their heads, legs, and
                  tail into their shells for protection. Turtles
                  that live on land have a high, domed shell.
                  Turtles that live in the water have flatter
                  shells. Some shells are plain black or
                  brown. Some shells are very colorful and
                  can have bright green, yellow, orange, or
                  red markings.

Turtle -   All turtles lay their eggs on land. A mother turtle digs a hole with her back feet. She covers the hole with dirt or sand. A sea turtle can lay 200 eggs at one time! The mother turtle leaves her eggs. Baby turtles must take care of themselves as soon as they are born!

Snake -   Hello! I am a snake. There are about 3,000 different kinds of snakes. Snakes do not have any legs, eyelids, or ear openings. Snakes live all over the world except in very cold places.

Zoologist #3 -   Some snakes are born from eggs. Some snakes grow within the mother's body. A mother snake will lay her eggs in the ground or inside a hollow log. She must find a way to keep the eggs warm and safe.

Snake -   Baby snakes are able to care for themselves as soon as they are born. Mother snakes do not take care of their babies.

Zoologist #2 -   Please tell us more.

Snake -

All snakes eat animals. Snakes do not eat plants. Snakes eat rabbits, lizards, mice, frogs, birds, and insects. Snakes must swallow their food whole. Sometimes snakes can go an entire month without eating any food!

Zoologist #3 - Snakes are <u>really</u> interesting animals! Did you know that some snakes hibernate during the winter? Some snakes hibernate alone, but others gather in groups of up to 100 snakes!

Snake - We snakes have many enemies including hawks, owls, and eagles. Possums and skunks dig up our eggs. Many people kill snakes because they think we are harmful. But snakes actually help people. Snakes eat rats and mice that may eat farmer's crops.

Zoologist #3 - Snakes have little protection against their enemies. A snake's coloring can help it blend in with its surroundings.

Zoologist #2 - Look! Here comes a crocodile! Please tell us all about crocodiles!

Crocodile -   I'd be glad to! There are about 20 kinds of alligators and crocodiles. Crocodiles and alligators live in or near water. We use our long tails for swimming.

Zoologist #3 -   Please tell us more.

Crocodile -   A mother crocodile lays her eggs in a hole. She will guard her nest for about 80 days until the eggs hatch. A mother crocodile carries her babies from the nest into the water. Baby crocodiles know how to swim as soon as they are born. Unlike some of my other reptile friends, baby crocodiles stay with their mothers for several months.

Zoologist #2 -   What do crocodiles eat?

Crocodiles -   Crocodiles eat ducks, turtles, snakes, and fish. After eating, we sit in the sun. Our scales help camouflage us.

Gila monster -   Hello! I am a Gila monster! I live in the deserts of the Southwestern United States. We sleep during the day because it is so hot. We come out at night to hunt. We Gila monsters need to be careful . . . an owl or snake may try to eat us!

Zoologist -   Gila monsters have very sharp teeth. To find food, a Gila monster touches its tongue on the ground. The Gila monster can tell if an insect is near. Gila monsters only bite people in self defense.

Gila monster -   Mother Gila monsters bury their eggs in the sand. The eggs will hatch in about five months. After hatching, baby Gila monsters must take care of themselves.

Zoologist #1 -   Gila monsters can grow to be two feet long and weigh up to 40 pounds. Gila monsters have bumpy, beadlike scales of black and orange. During the winter months, Gila monsters will remain in their underground homes.

Zoologist #2 -   Wow! We've sure learned a lot today about . . .

All -   Radical Reptiles!

Gila Monster -   The End.

Reptiles are covered with scales. They are cold-blooded. Reptiles lay eggs.

Kevin

- To begin your unit of study, provide your students with all kinds of books and magazines about reptiles. A booklist is included in this unit to help you. Check around . . . does someone in your community own a pet snake or turtle?! Is there a nearby pet store that sells snakes or turtles that would allow your class to visit?! You'd be surprised of the many resources available to you right in your community . . . just start asking! Opportunities for hands-on experiences will <u>truly</u> enhance your students' lives.

- For easier reading, be sure to highlight each reader's part. Do not announce the name of the script. As students begin reading the script, check to see if those students in the audience can identify the kinds of animals described in the script.

- During additional readings, post these questions on the board. Encourage students to listen <u>and</u> look . . . the answers can be found in the script!

  - How do reptiles differ from other animals?

  - Where can reptiles be found?

  - What are the 4 groups of reptiles?

  - Name 3 things that snakes eat.

  - Tell how a mother turtle lays her eggs.

- Encourage students to pose questions to one another. If you are looking for ways to build oral language skills in your students, here's one way to do it! Children <u>love</u> "playing teacher" and asking questions of one another. Students can write questions on 3x5 cards with the answers on the back of the cards. The cards can be assembled together and read and shared throughout this exciting unit of study.

- **Read! Read! Read!** Two of my favorite books about reptiles are sure to be <u>BIG</u> hits with your students. Reproducible pages for a classbook or for a mural are included in this unit. The books are _Snakes Are Hunters_ by Patricia Lauber (Harper Trophy, 1988.) and _Scaly Babies: Reptiles Growing Up_ by Ginny Johnston and Judy Cutchins (Morrow Junior Books, 1988.)

- **WRITE! WRITE! WRITE!** Here are a few quick ideas for writing that you may wish to try with your students. Have students do a, "Quick Write and Share" in their science journals. Tell students to quickly jot down some facts that they have learned from the script or from other materials. After a five minute writing period, have students read and share their stories with five other students. Be sure to include yourself in this activity.

- You may wish to have students' try writing from a reptiles' point of view. To begin, have students stretch out on the floor as you direct them by saying, "You are now a reptile. You can be a snake, crocodile, lizard, or any other kind of reptile. How does your body look? Are you searching for food? How do you protect yourself from your enemies?" Following this activity, have students write about their experiences. Action writing gives students focus. It gives them greater understanding of the subject being studied.

- **POETRY! POETRY! POETRY!** Taking off with the action writing format, have students write poems entitled, "Things To Do If You Are A Reptile". A few samples are shown below. Students love writing these! There are lots of opportunities for creative expression, vocabulary building and best of all, by interweaving this poetry activity into the content area of science, you are adding a richness and depth to your instructional environment.

Things To Do If You Are a Snake

- Slither along

- Flick out your tongue

- Watch out for hawks!

- Look for a tasty little mouse to eat.

- Hope that no one steps on you!

Things To Do If You Are A Gila Monster

- Sleep all day in some other animal's burrow

- Come out to hunt at night

- Search for insects

- Watch Out! A snake might eat me!

- Lay some eggs in the sand.

More Poetry Ideas!

- Your students will <u>love</u> making snake-shape poems. Students can write poems about snakes on a flattened paper plate in a circular pattern beginning on the outside and working towards the center. The plates are then cut into a spiral . The flip side of the snake poem can be colored to look like a specific kind of snake. The spiral-shaped snake poems can be hung in the classroom for a terrific display!

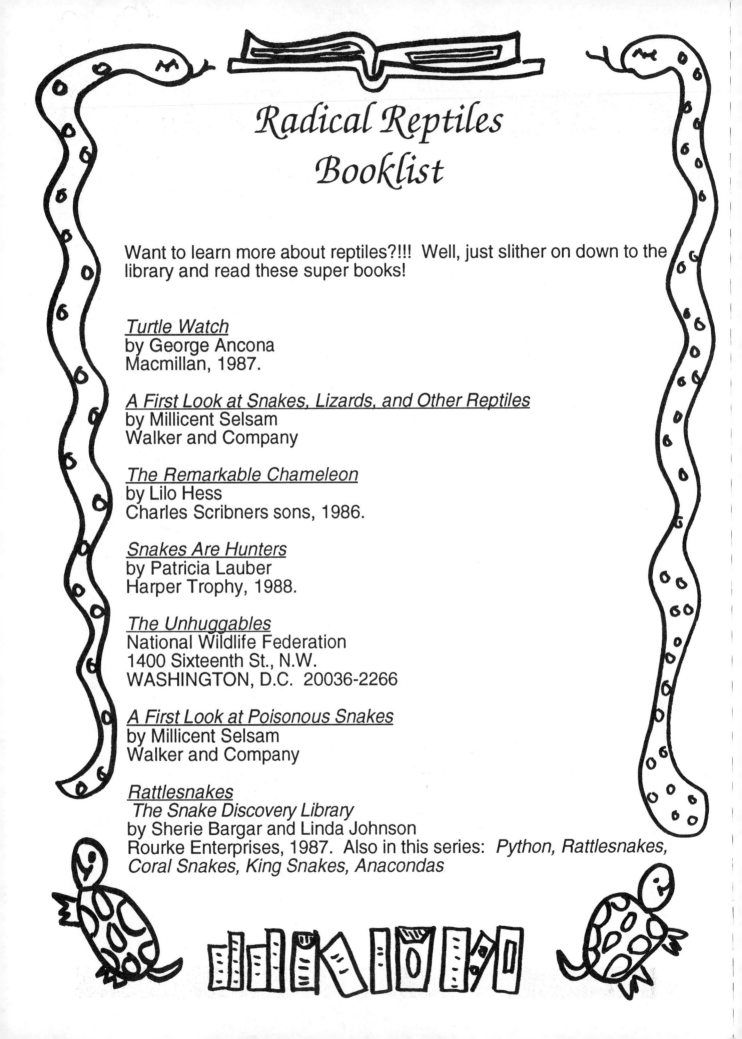

Radical Reptiles Booklist

Want to learn more about reptiles?!!! Well, just slither on down to the library and read these super books!

Turtle Watch
by George Ancona
Macmillan, 1987.

A First Look at Snakes, Lizards, and Other Reptiles
by Millicent Selsam
Walker and Company

The Remarkable Chameleon
by Lilo Hess
Charles Scribners sons, 1986.

Snakes Are Hunters
by Patricia Lauber
Harper Trophy, 1988.

The Unhuggables
National Wildlife Federation
1400 Sixteenth St., N.W.
WASHINGTON, D.C. 20036-2266

A First Look at Poisonous Snakes
by Millicent Selsam
Walker and Company

Rattlesnakes
 The Snake Discovery Library
by Sherie Bargar and Linda Johnson
Rourke Enterprises, 1987. Also in this series: *Python, Rattlesnakes, Coral Snakes, King Snakes, Anacondas*

Cooks in the Classroom

Bread Boas

Say, friends! Here's a fun recipe to try...and it's easy and good for you too!

Here's What You'll Need

- frozen bread dough, thawed
- 1 stick melted margarine
- green food coloring
- raisins
- q-tips

Here's What You Do:

- Divide the dough into small pieces and roll back and forth to make a snake
- Mix a few drops of green food coloring into the melted margarine
- Brush the margarine onto your Bread Boa
- Add raisins for eyes
- Bake at 350° for about 15 minutes...then eat...Yum!

Scaly Babies:
Reptiles Growing Up

by Ginny Johnston and Judy Cutchins

Hey, World! Take a look at me! I'm a baby _____. When I was born. When I _____. I weighed _____ when I was born. When I weigh _____ and _____ by _____. When I grow up I will _____.

Snakes Are Hunters

by Patricia Lauber

Did you know that snakes _____?

Let me tell you a few more facts that I know about snakes. _____

_____

by _____

Simply Sensational Snake Puppets

These slithery snakes are so much fun to make...all you'll need is an old tie, some felt and <u>LOTS</u> of imagination!

<u>Here's What You Do:</u>

Have an adult sew the narrow end of the tie closed. Fill the inside of the tie with polyester stuffing (available at any craft store). Use a yardstick or dowel to press the stuffing into the tie. When you've reached the end of the tie, ask a grown-up to sew the end shut using a diamond-shaped piece of felt. You can glue on googly eyes and a tongue.

Water Wise - All About Water Conservation

A Super Science Script
Written and Developed by Lisa Blau

Water Expert #1
Water Expert #2
Water Expert #3

Water Expert #4
Water Expert #5

Water Expert #1 - Good morning! We are here to tell you all about the earth's most precious resource . . .

All - WATER!

Water Expert #2 - Every form of life needs water in order to live.

Water Expert #4 - A tiny fish needs water . . .

Water Expert #5 - A tall tree needs water . . .

Water Expert #3 - <u>Everyone</u> needs . . .

All -   WATER!

Water Expert #2 -   People need water to drink because our bodies need water to stay healthy.

Water Expert #3 -   We also need water to make the crops grow so that we have food to eat.

Water Expert #4 -   People use water for taking baths, brushing their teeth, and washing their clothes.

Water Expert #1 -   Yes, everyone needs water.

Water Expert #2 -   We know that water is precious so we must find ways to save all the water that we can.

Water Expert #3 -   Now, you might be thinking . . .

Water Expert #5 -   But, I'm just a kid. What can I do to save water?

Water Expert #4 -   Well, we're here to tell you . . .

All -   PLENTY!

Water Expert #1 -   If you turn off the running water when
                     you brush your teeth . . .

All -   You can save 35 gallons of water in
                     one week!

Water Expert #3 -   If you take a shorter shower . . .

All -   You can save 75 gallons of water in
                     one week!

Water Expert #3 -   You can help Mom or Dad fix leaky
                     faucets and put water savers in your
                     toilets.

Water Expert #5 -   A plastic bottle filled with pebbles will
                     do the job!

Water Expert #4 -   Never play in sprinklers if your town is
                     having a water shortage.

Water Expert #1 -   Sure, it's tons of fun . . .

Water Expert #2 -   You will use over 10 gallons of
                     water in only one minute!

Water Expert #3 -   By trying some of these tricks, you
                     and your family can help save lots of
                     water.

Water Expert #1 - We have to work together to save water and to keep our water clean and safe.

Water Expert #2 - There is a lot that we can do to keep our oceans, lakes, and rivers clean.

Water Expert #3 - Sure! It's easy! Be sure that you never litter near water.

Water Expert #5 - You can write letters to your congressman asking to pass laws to help protect our lakes, rivers, and oceans.

Water Expert #4 - Water is precious. What can you do to help save water?

Water Expert #1 - Make sure that the faucet is turned off all the way. Don't leave it dripping. . .

Water Expert #2 - Every drop counts you know!

Water Expert #3 - Don't use more water than you really need. You really don't need to fill your bathtub up all the way when you take a bath.

Water Expert #4 -   You should use a broom . . . not the hose to clean your driveway or sidewalks.

Water Expert #5 -   And how many of you like to help out by washing the car? Well, be sure to save water when you wash the car.

Water Expert #2 -   It's easy . . . just use a bucket to wash the car, and only use the hose to rinse it off.

All -   We hope that you will be water wise and save lots of water. We know you can do it!

Water Expert #3 -   The End.

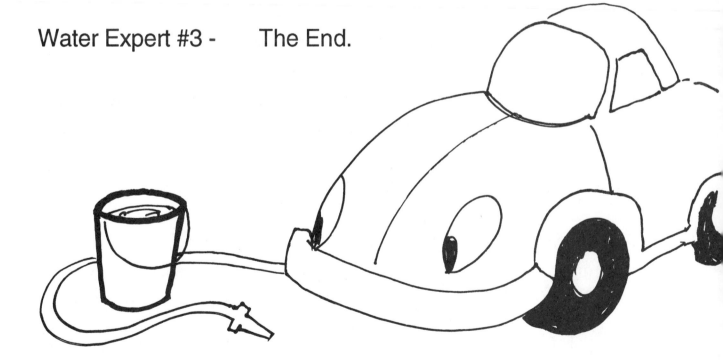

- As a pre-reading activity, ask students to write facts on the water drop pattern found in this unit. Younger students could simply draw pictures of the different ways that people use water. The completed water drop pages can be read and shared and then hung on a mural.

- After students have read the script, a second set of water drop pages can be passed out. This time instruct students to write (or draw pictures) about new facts on water learned from the script. These completed pages can also be hung on the mural.

- Students often have difficulty understanding the fact that while the earth is covered with more water than land, many regions experience droughts. As a related science experiment, plant bean seeds and water one pot with tap water and the other pot with salt water. Have students use the Science Journal Response Page included in this unit as a means for recording the results of the experiment.

- Is your city-state experiencing a water shortage? Have students keep a sharp eye in their local papers for news about the drought. Keep a scrapbook of these articles and discuss. Incidental science is science at its best! You can also have students write letters requesting materials and information from your city's water department. Wow! Writing with a purpose! Many water companies have booklets, coloring books and even guest speakers available to schools. You may hit the jack-pot!

- Water pollution is a very serious problem. Again, use the news as means for discussing science topics. Encourage students to look for news articles pertaining to water pollution. Discuss ways that we can all help fight water pollution. You may also wish to show the effects of pollutants by having students water plants that have been tainted with motor oil and detergents. You will need three healthy plants to begin this experiment. One plant will be the control plant.

Children should water this plant with <u>fresh water</u>. Plant Number Two should be watered each day with a cup containing <u>one-half water</u> and one-half motor oil. Plant Number Three should be watered each day with a cup containing <u>one-half water and one-half detergent</u>.

- Begin this experiment by telling children that water pollution is a very serious problem. Children can talk about some of the ways that man has polluted our water. Explain that you will use one plant as a "control" plant to show what happens to plants when they receive healthy water. Have students make predictions about what may happen to each plant. An excellent book to share at this time is <u>Prince William</u> by Gloria Rand. It describes the effects of the Valdez oil spill.

- Students can record the results of this experiment on the Science Journal Response Page included in this unit.

- Be sure to keep your healthy plant in a prominent place in your classroom to remind students of the importance of keeping our water supplies free from pollutants.

- MATH! MATH! MATH! The script gives information regarding the amount of water it takes to perform daily functions such as brushing one's teeth or taking a shower. People use an average of 90 gallons of water per day. As a math activity, have students estimate the number of gallons of water that they use each day.

- MORE MATH! Have students use the Water Usage Chart personal record form included in this unit to determine how much water each child uses on a daily basis. These pages can be completed by individual students or by an entire family. Look for ways that the activities in this book can be used by students at home thereby strengthening the home-school connection. Quite obviously, any of the scripts can be sent home for families to read and perform together. You'll be amazed at the positive feedback that you'll recieve when you send home the scripts, recipes, or science experiment pages found in this resourcebook.

- READ! READ! READ! There are <u>many</u> excellent books about water to add to your unit of study. Be sure to contact your local department of water for your city as they may be able to supply you with all kinds of terrific resources to add to your unit. Here are a few of the books my students enjoyed most:

  - *The Magic School Bus at the Water Works*
    by Joanna Cole
    Scholastic Publishers

  - *What to Do When Your Mom or Dad Say . . . Turn off the Water and Lights*
    by Joy Berry
    Children's Press

  - *Water for the World*
    by Franklin Branley
    Crowell Publishers

  - *The Science Project Book of Water*
    by Steve Parker
    Marshall Cavendish Corporation

  - *Wonderful Water*
    by Bobbie Kalman and Janine Schaub
    Crabtree Publishing Company

- And finally, you'll find two WONDERFUL "Family Fun Super Science Experiment Pages" included in this unit. Send the page home so that your students can share the exciting results with their families. Be sure to ask parents to send in photos of families engaged in the experiments so that you can post the photos in a prominent spot in your classroom. What an <u>easy</u> and <u>rewarding</u> way to strengthen the home-school connection!

- Wait! There's more!!! Have students design water conservation signs by using the "Artfully Quick and Easy" project included in this unit. Have students brainstorm possible water-saving slogans and then color the door knob signs with felt pens. Water-saving facts could be written by the students on the back side of the door knob signs.

- Noted author Michelle Koch has created a <u>lovely</u> book about the importance of conserving water. In addition, she gives many facts about animals that make their homes in water including penguins, seals, otters and turtles. A <u>wonderful</u> companion to your unit on water conservation. The book is entitled <u>World Water Watch</u> (ISBN #0-688-11465-2). You can order this book by calling One From The Heart Educational Resources (206) 885-7565.

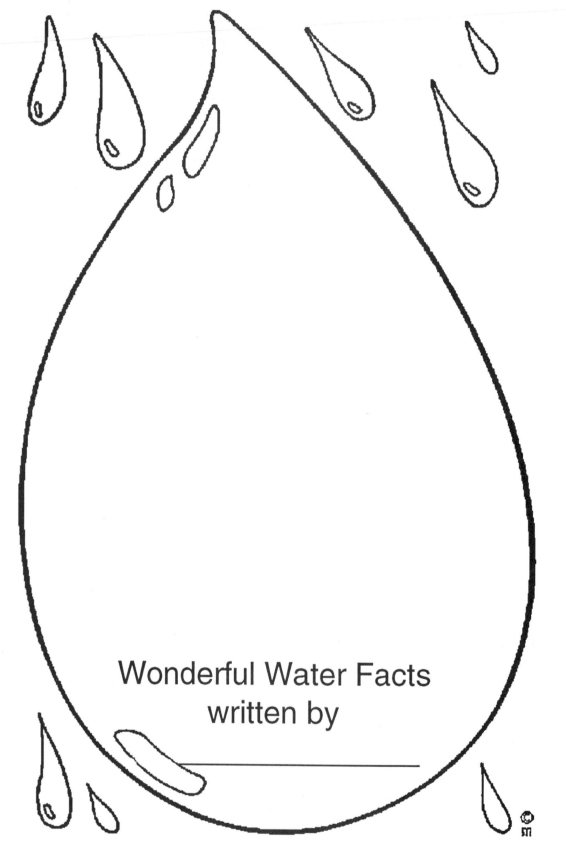

Wonderful Water Facts
written by

_____

Note: Use these patterns to create a mural or class book about water facts.

Super Science Journal Page

Question: What effect does salt water have on plant growth?

Hypothesis: _____

_____

Procedures: _____

_____

Results: _____

_____

Conclusion: _____

_____

Draw pictures to show the results of your experiment here ↓

Super Science Journal Page

Question: What effect do oil and detergent have on plant growth?

Hypothesis: _____

_____

Procedures: _____

_____

Results: _____

_____

Conclusion: _____

_____

* **Super Science Challenge:** Write a list of ways that we

can help stop water pollution. <u>OR</u> draw pictures of

your three plants at the end of your experiment.

My Water Usage Chart

by _____

Hello Super Scientists and Water Conservationists!

Look at the chart below and then record how much water you use in one day. Be sure to add up your total.

Shower	5 gallons
Brushing Teeth	3 gallons
Washing Hands	3 gallons
Flushing Toilet	3 gallons
Washing Face	1 1/2 gallons
Washing Dishes by Hand	35 gallons

I Used Water To: **Amount Used**

_____   _____gallons

_____   _____gallons

_____   _____gallons

_____   _____gallons

                                                    TOTAL: _____

_____

 Super Brain's Challenge: Make a list of ways that you can conserve water on the back of this page.

Save Water
Door Knob Sign

Say kids!!! Here's a FUN activity to try!!! Think of a slogan that tells why we should save water such as, "Don't Be a Drip...Save Every Drop!" Write your slogan on the Door Knob Sign using bubble letters or other fancy print styles. Be sure to add bright illustrations! Cut out your Door Knob Sign and hang it where everyone can see it!

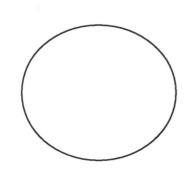

Family Fun!
SUPER SCIENCE EXPERIMENT

Question: Can you lift an ice cube out of a glass of water without touching the ice cube with your hands?!!

Here are the materials that you will need:

a glass of cold water
a piece of string - about 6 inches long
one ice cube
salt

Directions:

Place the ice cube into the glass of water. Now place one end of your string across the ice cube and then sprinkle a small amount of salt onto the ice cube. Wait ten seconds...now try lifting the ice cube...WOW!

Here's Why it Works:

The salt lowered the freezing temperature of the ice cube and caused the ice cube to melt. As the ice cube melts, a bit of water forms on top of it and your string sticks to it. This explains why in areas where it snows, salt is used to clear the roads.

*   *Attention all super scientists...If you'd like to try more science experiments at home check out <u>Science Experiments You Can Eat</u> by Vicki Cobb...It's lots of fun and tasty too!!!*

Feathered Friends

A Super Science Script
Written and Developed by Lisa Blau

| Owl | Ostrich | Trumpeter Swan |
| Pelican | Hummingbird | Eagle |

Trumpeter Swan - Ko-hoh! I am a Trumpeter Swan. I want you to meet some of my feathered friends.

Ostrich - Hello! I am an ostrich. I am the largest of all birds. I live in Africa.

Hummingbird - I'm one of the world's smallest birds. I am a hummingbird. Hummingbirds can be as small as a bee. The humming sound that we make comes from the vibration of our wings.

Eagle - Some people call me the "King of Birds". That's because eagles are symbols of strength, courage, and power. I am the national bird of the United States.

Pelican - Well, hello! I am a pelican. I have a king-sized throat that I use to catch fish. I'm very big. I measure 50 inches from my bill to my tail.

Owl -  Whoo! Whoo! I am a Great Horned Owl. I do not really have horns. I have large tufts of feathers on the top of my head that look like horns. I am the largest of all owls. I am 2 1/2 feet in height.

Trumpeter Swan - These are my feathered friends. They will tell you some interesting facts about themselves . . . so, Ko-hoh! Ko-hoh! Listen up, bird lovers!

Eagle - There are 59 different kinds of eagles. We eagles can be found all over the world except for ice-covered Antarctica.

Hummingbird -  Hummingbirds can be found from the tip of South America all the way to Alaska. Some hummingbirds migrate in spring. They may travel over 2,500 miles each way!

Owls -

There are about 133 different kinds of owls. Like our friend the eagle, we are found all over the world, except for Antarctica. My friend the Elf Owl makes his home inside a cactus in the hot, hot desert.

Ostrich -

Desert . . . did someone say desert?! Ostriches live in the desert plains of Africa. We live in large groups and we move around all the time in search of food.

Pelican -

Food . . . glorious food! That reminds me . . . I'm hungry! We pelicans live near water and eat fish. We can easily scoop up lots of fish in our large pouches.

Trumpeter Swan -

Swans live on every continent of the world except for Africa. Trumpeter Swans are the world's largest swans. We were named for our loud voices. We like to eat insects, water beetles, and shrimp.

Trumpeter Swan - If you have ever wondered why birds do not get wet, it is because we have a special oil that covers our feathers. We use our bills to rub this oil into our feathers. This is called preening. Preening our feathers makes them waterproof.

Hummingbird - Hummingbirds eat all the time. We eat insects, but our favorite food is nectar. A hummingbird might sip nectar from over 1,000 flowers each day.

Eagles -

Hmpf! Nectar from a 1,000 flowers wouldn't be the kind of food we eagles want. Eagles eat insects, fish, reptiles, other birds, and mammals. We are strong and powerful hunters with keen eyesight, sharp claws, and a strong beak. We are also very skilled and very fast fliers.

Owl - Well, owls are excellent hunters too, friend Eagle. Just like the eagle, owls have sharp claws and strong beaks. Our huge eyes help us to see in the dark. I can hear a mouse scampering over dry leaves from far away.

Owl - When I fly, I can glide in silence when I hunt for food. Owls eat snakes, mice and other small animals. And my once I catch my food, I eat it whole!

Ostrich - We ostriches have very poor smell and hearing, but very sharp eyesight. We can see over long distances because of our long necks. We like to search for food with zebras and antelopes. Together, we can be on the look-out for our enemies.

Trumpeter Swan - Who are your enemies, Friend Ostrich?

Ostrich - Our main enemies are lions, leopards, and wild dogs. Since we cannot fly, we must run away from our enemies. We can outrun most animals because even though we are very big, we are quick runners. Ostriches can run as fast as 40-50 miles per hour.

Eagle - Wow! Now that's fast! An eagle's greatest enemy is man. People cut down trees and took away our homes. People polluted rivers and lakes and killed the fish that we eat.

Trumpeter Swan - Man is one of the trumpeter swan's enemies too. There are laws to protect us. Bears and coyotes might try to eat our eggs, but the father swan will chase away any enemies by flapping his wings.

Owl -  Man is one of the owl's enemies. People hunt owls or poison them with chemicals that pollute the land. Some owls will attack other owls. A sleeping owl may be caught by a hungry wolf or leopard.

Pelican - People are the pelican's enemy too. People pollute the water and poison the fish that we eat. Some people frighten pelicans from their nests. There are laws to protect pelicans.

Hummingbird -  Even though we can fly very fast, we hummingbirds must be on the alert for our enemies. Our enemies are falcons, dragonflies and hawks. Since a hummingbird can fly up, down, forward, and backwards, we can sometimes escape from our enemies.

Pelican -

Wow! You hummingbirds are real acrobats! We pelicans are very graceful in the air. Our nine-foot wings help us glide through the air. On land, we waddle like ducks with our big, webbed feet.

Owl -

I can glide through the air too, friend Pelican. My flight feathers are not stiff like most birds. Mine are soft and fringed at the edges. Owls can glide . . . and we can do it <u>silently</u>!

Ostrich -

Gee, I wish I could glide like you, friend Owl. We ostriches are just too big and too heavy to fly. We also have tiny wings. It's a good thing that we can run fast in the sand.

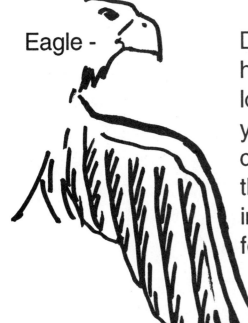

Eagle -

Did you know that my wings are like a human arm? The bones in my wings look much the same as the bones in your arm. The tip of my wings are covered with primary feathers. I use these feathers to help me glide along in strong winds. I also use these feathers for takeoffs and landing.

Trumpeter Swan -   Ko-hoh! Ko-hoh! I have long, strong wings too! My wings can span 8 feet from tip to tip. Ko-hoh! Ko-hoh! It was fun learning all about our feathered friends today.

Owl -   And if you'd like to be a wise old bird like me . . . why not visit the library and read all about the world's beautiful birds?!

Ostrich -   Afterall, there are over 9,000 kinds of birds in the world for you to read about!

Eagle -   Wow, that's a lot of feathered friends!

Trumpeter Swan -   Ko - hoh - Ko - hoh!

All -   The End

• As a pre-reading activity, ask students to name their favorite kinds of birds and to tell any facts that they know about their "feathered friends". A Knowledge Chart could be used to record student responses.

• Review the script so that students become familiar with any new or unfamiliar words. Create a "Birds Words List" by writing down words related to the study of birds. This list will prove helpful when students are asked to write about birds and the facts that they have learned.

• After reading the script, ask students the following questions:

Listen and Learn:

• Where do ostriches live?

• What bird migrates 2,500 miles in search of food?

• What bird can fly silently?

• Why do hummingbirds hum?

• What does an owl eat?

• Have students re-read the script if they are unable to answer any of your questions. Encourage them to look and listen for key information.

Note: If this script proves to be too difficult for your students, give it to the teacher in a higher grade level. Ask her students to come in a read the script to your class. You may also wish to ask for some assistance from your sixth grade buddies when presenting this script to your class.

• Play the "Feathered Friends Game" with your students. Simply pin pictures of different kinds of birds onto the students' backs. Everyone walks about the room asking questions about themselves such as, "Where do I live?" or "What do I eat?" until the students determine their "birds" identities. Use the bird pictures found in this unit.

- For added fun, students can make decorative headbands to wear while reading the script. Simply reproduce the pictures of birds included in this unit for your students. After the pictures have been colored in with felt pen, staple individual pictures onto a sentence strip and staple the strip together to form a headband. Your students will LOVE these!

- Read! Read! Read! After lunch you can share E.B. White's classic, _The Trumpet of the Swan_. What a marvelous way to integrate science and literature. Extend the learning by having students keep a journal. Students can draw pictures of Louis and his adventures as well as write information about trumpeter swans. The journals will prove to be a special keepsake for your students. Farley Mowat's _An Owl in the Family_ is also a perfect read-aloud for your unit on birds.

- Read! Read! Read! Use the accompanying booklist to help create a "Bird Center" in your classroom. This specially designated area will feature books about birds as well as magazines and other resources. Encourage students to bring in books, pictures, nests, feathers . . . ANYTHING that they have to add to your special learning center.

- Math! Math! Math! Graph favorite kinds of birds using the six birds presented in this script OR compare wingspans of various kinds of birds (owl 9 feet, swan 8 feet) to the arm span of your students. What other statistics could you compare?! The possibilities are endless!

- Sing! Sing! Sing! Write "Piggy Back" songs about your favorite birds! Piggy Back songs are composed by taking the tune from a classic children's song such as "Skip to My Lou" or "Did You Ever See a Lassie?" and simply writing your own words. What a marvelous way to bring science, reading, writing, and music together. Two songs composed by my students can be found on the following page. Why not top off your performance by having students sing their newly composed "Piggy Back" songs after they have read the script for another class?!! What a fun activity!

Did You Ever See An Ostrich?

(sung to Did You Ever See a Lassie?)

Did you ever see an ostrich
an ostrich, and ostrich.
Did you ever see an
ostrich running across
the sand?

Eagles are Soaring

(sung to Skip to My Lou)

Eagles are soaring in the sky.
Eagles are soaring in the sky.
Eagles are soaring in the sky.
They use their primary
feathers to help them fly.

- Wait! There's one more egg-citing activity to try with your unit about birds!!! You'll find a reproducible "Family Fun Super Science Experiment Page" for students to try at home with their families. All of your work about birds will no doubt lead to some discussion about eggs, so here's a quick, easy, and <u>educational</u> activity to try!

- A <u>darling</u> sequined swan pin will make the perfect gift for someone special in your students' lives. This quick and easy art project will also be a terrific way to bring closure on your unit about birds.

- A special, "Family Fun Super Science Experiment Page" is included in this unit. This experiment will demonstrate how birds are able to stay dry while they swim as the Trumpeter Swan described in the script. Be sure to encourage families to take photos of themselves engaged in the experiment. These are fun to display in the classroom or in your classroom or school newsletter. By the way, the family science experiment pages make <u>great</u> homework assignments!

SUPER SCIENCE EXPERIMENT

Question: Can you remove the shell of an egg without cracking it?!!

Here are the materials that you will need:

one uncooked egg
one glass
vinegar

Directions:

Gently place the uncooked egg into a glass full of vinegar. Observe the egg for a few days. On the third day, remove the egg from the glass. What does it feel like?!

Here's Why it Works:

An egg shell is made of calcium. The vinegar is an acid. The vinegar dissolves the calcium. What's left to hold the egg together is the skin or bladder. Look for the skin under the shell the next time you peel a hard boiled egg. What an egg-citing science experiment!!!

SAY SUPER SCIENTISTS...FOR MORE EGG-CITING SCIENCE FUN BE SURE TO READ EGG-DROP DAY BY HARRIET ZIEFERT. YOU CAN HAVE GREAT FUN TRYING TO MAKE YOUR OWN PARACHUTES FOR AN EGG!!!

Family Fun!
SUPER SCIENCE EXPERIMENT

Question: Why don't birds get wet when they swim?

Here are the materials that you will need:

2 feathers	newspapers
salad oil	2 small bowls
water	paper towels

Here's What You Do:

Spread newspapers over your work space to keep it clean. Pour a small amount of salad oil in one bowl and water in the other bowl. Dip your fingers into the oil and run your fingers back and forth across one of the feathers. Do this several times so that the feather is coated with oil. Wipe your hands clean on the paper towels. Now dip your hands into the water and sprinkle water on your feather. Do the same with the untreated feather. Tell what happened to each of your feathers.

Here's Why it Works:

Your oiled feather did not get wet because oil and water do not mix. Birds have oil glands near their tails. They rub oil onto their feathers with their bills or beaks. This is called preening. Birds will spend hours preening so that their feathers are covered with oil. Water rolls right off of the oily feathers and the birds stay dry whenever they go for a swim.

♥ If you'd like to try more super science experiments, be sure to read Janice Van Cleave's 200 Gooey, Slippery and Slimy Science Experiments. It's totally cool!

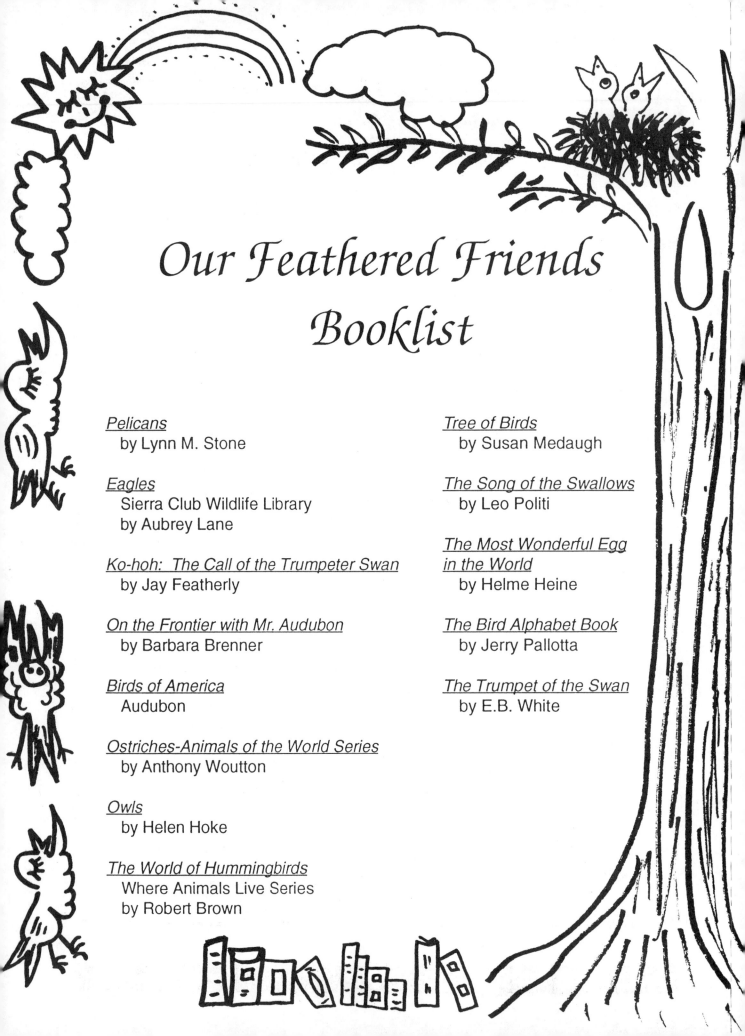

Our Feathered Friends Booklist

Pelicans
by Lynn M. Stone

Eagles
Sierra Club Wildlife Library
by Aubrey Lane

Ko-hoh: The Call of the Trumpeter Swan
by Jay Featherly

On the Frontier with Mr. Audubon
by Barbara Brenner

Birds of America
Audubon

Ostriches-Animals of the World Series
by Anthony Woutton

Owls
by Helen Hoke

The World of Hummingbirds
Where Animals Live Series
by Robert Brown

Tree of Birds
by Susan Medaugh

The Song of the Swallows
by Leo Politi

The Most Wonderful Egg in the World
by Helme Heine

The Bird Alphabet Book
by Jerry Pallotta

The Trumpet of the Swan
by E.B. White

Feathered Friends
Sequined Swan Pin

Here's a fun art project that can be given to someone special. It's a lovely handmade gift...and that's the best kind of gift to give because it's made with LOVE.

Here's What You'll Need:

- one gray piece of felt
- one white piece of felt
- glitter and sequins (silver, gold)
- black sequins for eyes
- white glue
- pinking shears
- tagboard
- safety pins

Here's What You Do:

Trace the patterns onto the tagboard and cut out the patterns. Now trace the patterns onto the felt. Use gray felt for the head and white felt for the body and wing. Glue the felt pieces onto the tagboard and glue the head to the body and the wing to the body as well. Rub glue across the wing and body and sprinkle with sequins and glitter. Carefully add one black sequin for the swan's eye. Let dry, then attach a safety pin to the back of your sequined swan. What a <u>lovely</u> gift for someone that you love!

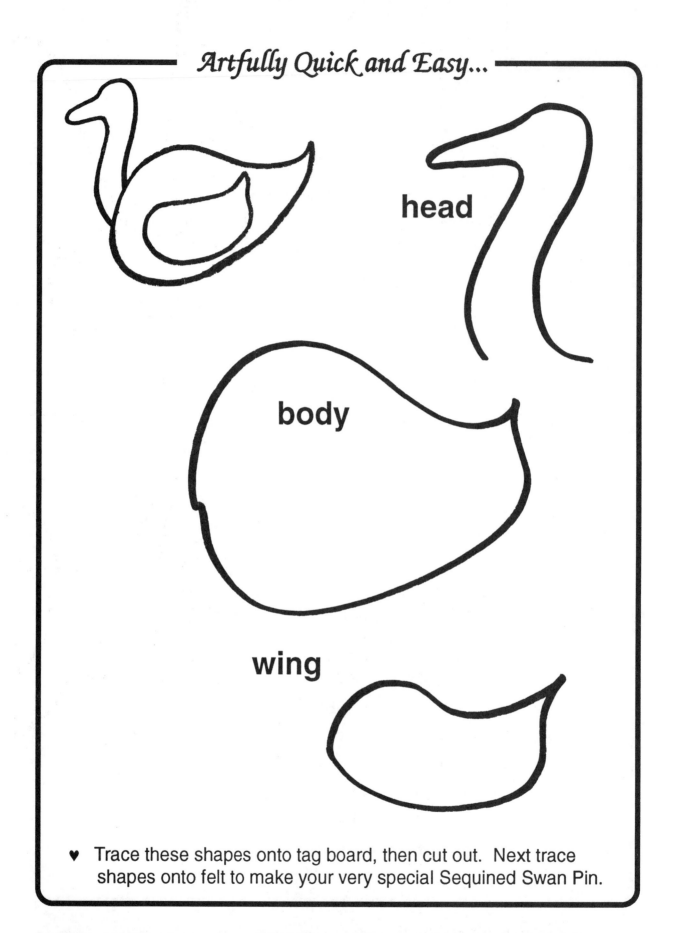

head

body

wing

♥ Trace these shapes onto tag board, then cut out. Next trace
  shapes onto felt to make your very special Sequined Swan Pin.

Reader's Headbands
for the
Feathered Friends Script

hummingbird

swan

owl

penguin

Reader's Headbands for the Feathered Friends Script

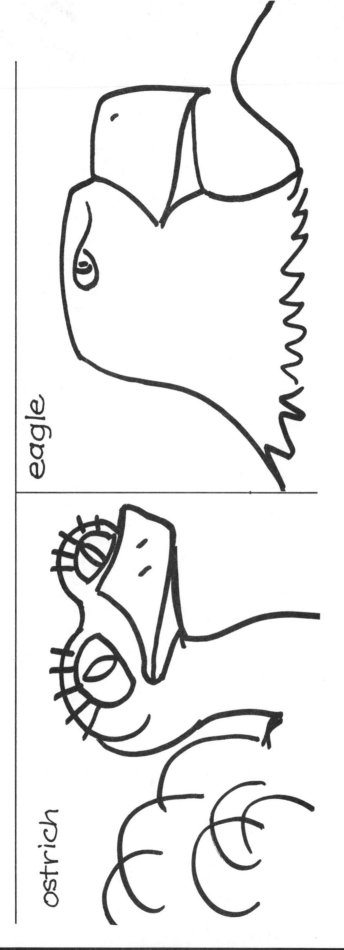

eagle

ostrich

Volcanos

A Super Science Script
Written and Developed by Lisa Blau

Geologist #1
Geologist #2
Geologist #3

Geologist #4
Geologist #5
Geologist #6

Geologist #1 - Good morning! We are a group of geologists. We'd like to tell you all about volcanos.

Geologist #3 - Geologists are scientists who study the earth. We study all about earthquakes and volcanos. Our work is <u>very</u> interesting.

Geologist #5 - Our earth is made up of many layers of rock. The top layer is called the crust.

Geologist #6 - The middle layer of the earth is called the mantle. The center part of our earth is called the core.

Geologist #2 -   Deep within the earth there is hot rock called magma. The rock is so hot that it melts just like a candy bar on a hot summer's day.

Geologist #4 -   Most magma forms 50 to 100 miles beneath the earth's surface.

Geologist #5 -   When the rock melts, it makes a gas that mixes with the hot melted rock.

Geologist #3 -   The magma rises to the earth's surface because it is lighter than the solid rock around it.

Geologist #1 -   Volcanos are formed when the magma pushes through cracks and holes on the earth's surface. This force is so strong it can blow off the top of a mountain.

Geologist #5 -   Three kinds of material can erupt from a volcano. They are...

Geologist #6 -   Lava.

Geologist #1 -   Rock Fragments.

Geologist #2 -   And gases.

Geologist #4 - When the magma reaches the earth's surface, it is called lava. Lava can move down the sides of the volcano very quickly. Lava is <u>very</u> hot.

Geologist #5 - Volcanos also push out volcanic ash. Volcanic ash is made of very tiny rock fragments.

Geologist #6 - Sometimes volcanic ash mixes with water in a stream and forms a dangerous mudflow.

Geologist #3 - A mudflow can move very fast. It can destroy everything in its path.

Geologist #4 - There are thousands of volcanos all over the earth. There are volcanos in the United States. Some are active, some are not.

Geologist #5 - Did you know that lava poured over the walls of the Grand Canyon over one million years ago?

Geologist #2 - Let's find out about one of the most famous volcanos in the United States.

Geologist #6 -   On May 18, 1980 at 8:32 A.M., Mount St. Helens in the state of Washington erupted.

Geologist #1 -   People living 200 miles away heard the blast. Steam, gas, and ashes were thrown into the air.

Geologist #3 -   The ash mixed with water from Spirit Lake and nearby rivers making a huge mudflow.

Geologist #2 -   The mudflow destroyed everything in its path.

Geologist #4 -   The volcano blew down millions of trees. Huge pine trees fell to the ground like toothpicks.

Geologist #5 -   Scientists do not know when Mount St. Helens or any other volcanos may erupt again.

Geologist #1 -   Being a geologist and studying the wonders of the earth is an exciting job.

Geologist #3 -   Wow! We've learned a lot about volcanos today. It's fun learning about our amazing earth.

Geologist #4 -   I'll say! I had a real <u>BLAST</u> learning about volcanos.

Geologist #6 -   We hope you enjoyed our presentation.

All -   The End.

- Draw a model of the earth to show its layers prior to reading the script with your students. You may also choose to make a sketch of a volcano so that students are familiar with the terms used in the script. You can write words such as mantle, lava, magma, crust and core onto index cards and have students place the cards next to these features on your drawings. Photos of the eruption of Mount St. Helens would also greatly add to this pre-reading lesson. A good resource for full color photos can be found in <u>Volcano - The Eruption of Mount St. Helens</u> published by Longview Publishing Company. Card Catalog #80-82434.

- Have students create a classbook based upon information that they have learned either from the script or from other sources. Two favorite children's books about volcanos that your students will enjoy are:

  - <u>Volcanos and Earthquakes</u>
    by Martyn Bramwell
    Franklin Watts Publishers, 1986.

  - <u>Volcano: The Eruption and Healing of Mount St. Helens</u>
    by Patricia Lauber
    Bradbury Press, 1988.

- Students can work with a partner to report on information about volcanos. The partners can also collaborate on an illustration. Student work can be mounted on construction paper and laminated. The laminated pages can be placed into a plastic-ring binder <u>OR</u> you may consider creating a classbook in the shape of a volcano. Simply cut a tagboard cover into the shape of a volcano and ask one of your students to add some illustrations. The value of creating science classbooks is based upon research. Research has shown that children learn more effectively when instruction is integrated into several subjects of the curriculum at the same time.

By using this interdisciplinary approach, you will help your students understand the relationships of one discipline to another, and it's also great fun for the children. What more can a teacher hope for than excited, motivated students who are having fun while they learn?!

- Looking for more ideas to share with your students?!! Send away for Kids Discover Magazine...it's <u>GREAT</u>! Ask for Volume 3, Issue 6 on volcanos.

Mail Orders to: Kids Discover Magazine
                                170 Fifth Avenue
                                New York, New York 10010

The individual issues sell for $3.00 per copy. A full year's subscription costs $17.95 for one year. There are special rates available for group orders. Other single issue titles include Oceans, Weather, Space, Rain Forests...and many, many more! Why not ask PTA to give the gift of a subscription to your whole school?!

- Cooks in the Classroom! Your students will simply explode with enthusiasm when you let them prepare some Strawberry Volcano Cookies as a culmination to your unit on volcanos.

Family Fun!

SUPER SCIENCE EXPERIMENT

Question: Can you make a volcano in a bottle?

Here's What You'll Need:

one plastic dishpan   vinegar
one cup hot water   baking soda
measuring cup   empty salad dressing bottle
tablespoon

Here's What You Do:

Place the bottle into the dishpan. Pour the hot water into the bottle. Add one tablespoon of baking soda and one half cup of vinegar to your bottle. Now you can watch a "volcano" erupt right before your eyes!

Here's Why it Works:

When you added the baking soda and vinegar to the water, you created a chemical reaction. A gas called carbon dioxide was created and it began to expand. The carbon dioxide gas is lighter than water, so it pushed itself up to the top of the bottle. Magma inside a volcano is just like the water in the bottle. Magma erupts because gases expand and push the magma out of the volcano.

*   ATTENTION SUPER SCIENTISTS! BE SURE TO READ SEYMOUR SIMON'S MARVELOUS BOOK CALLED <u>VOLCANOES</u>. YOU'LL LOVE IT!!

Strawberry Volcano Cookies

2/3 C. butter
1/3 C. sugar
2 egg yolks
1 tsp. vanilla

1 1/2 C. flour
2 egg whites, slightly beaten
1/3 C. strawberry jam
3/4 C. finely chopped walnuts

Cream butter and sugar until fluffy. Add egg <u>yolks</u> and vanilla and beat well. Slowly add flour, mixing well. Shape into small balls, dip into egg whites and roll into nuts. Place one inch apart on a <u>greased</u> cookie sheet. Press down centers with your thumb. Bake at 350o for 15 minutes. Cool slightly then add jam to centers. These cookies are OVERFLOWING with flavor! Y-U-M-M-Y!!!

Dazzling Dinosaurs

A Super Science Script
Written and Developed by Lisa Blau

Ethan

Paleontologist #1   Tyrannosaurus Rex
Paleontologist #2   Diplodocus
Paleontologist #3   Brachiosaurus

Paleontologist #1 -   Good morning! Welcome to our presentation called...

All -   Dazzling Dinosaurs!

Diplodocus -   Hello there! I am a Diplodocus. The Diplodocus was the longest dinosaur that ever lived.

Paleontologist #3 -   That's right! Our friend Dippy was longer than 5 or 6 cars all lined up in a row!

Diplodocus -   The Diplodocus was a plant eater. A Diplodocus spent most of its time eating.

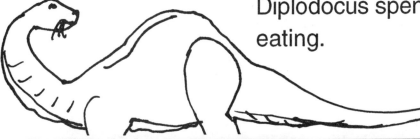

Paleontologist #2 -   Can anyone name the heaviest dinosaur?

Paleontologist #1 -   Oh, that's an easy one! The Brachiosaurus weighed over 100,000 pounds. This huge dinosaur was as heavy as ten elephants!

Brachiosaurus -   Hello! I am a Brachiosaurus. A Brachiosaurus was a plant eater. The Brachiosaurus was so heavy that it spent most of its time in the water.

Paleontologist #3 -   Can you name a dinosaur that walked on two feet?

Tyrannosaurus Rex -   That would be me, the Tyrannosaurus Rex. The Tyrannosaurus Rex was a meat eating dinosaur. We attacked plant eaters.

Paleontologist #1 -   What else can you tell us, Rex?

Tyrannosaurus Rex - The Tyrannosaurus Rex had long, sharp teeth. In fact, our teeth were over 6 inches long. We were excellent fighters. We had sharp teeth, sharp claws, and the ability to run very fast. We were <u>very</u> ferocious.

Paleontologist #3 - Wow! We've really learned a lot about the amazing animals of long ago!

Paleontologist #2 - I'll say! Who knows, maybe I'll go to college someday and become a paleontologist!

Paleontologist #3 - That would be really great! Maybe they'd name a dinosaur after you!

Paleontologist #1 - We hope you enjoyed our presentation.

Tyrannosaurus Rex - The End.

Neil

- Use the exceptional book, <u>The News About Dinosaurs</u> by Patricia Lauber to add to your study. Use the accompanying classbook page in this unit for student responses. Although the book is quite long and wordy, students will be amazed to learn how paleontologists are always finding new and exciting information about dinosaurs. Be sure to encourage students to read the newspapers for any articles about paleontologists and their discoveries. Who knows, maybe this book will inspire a child in your class to become a paleontologist!

- Create a Dazzling Dinosaur Science Symposium Center! Place some models or pictures of dinosaurs in your science center for students to work with during free time. Provide a set of 3x5 cards that contain the following questions. These questions were designed to emphasize students' higher level thinking skills along with honing their observational skills.

1. Look at the dinosaur models. Place the plant-eating dinosaurs into one group. Place the meat-eating dinosaurs in another group. Now describe the differences between these two groups of dinosaurs.

2. Look closely at the dinosaur models. Describe how some dinosaurs were able to protect themselves from their enemies.

3. Place the dinosaur models in order according to size from smallest to largest. Tell what each kind of dinosaur ate.

4. Select the dinosaur that you like the best. Place the dinosaur model in front of you and write a description of your favorite dinosaur. Now make a sketch of your dinosaur. Share your work with a friend.

Note: When designing a science program for your students, it is vitally important to provide students with hands-on experiences that will enable children to make observations, gather data, write, and carry-out analysis. A science center with extended activities can <u>greatly</u> enhance your science program. You will inspire learning by preparing activities much like the one described above.

- After reading the script, students can record the facts that they have learned on the, "Dinosaur Data Sheet" included in this unit. Student pages can be compiled into a classbook <u>OR</u> students can write out a page for each of the dinosaurs described in the script and staple together to create a "DINO-MITE" personal book to take home and read to family members.

- <u>Cooks in the Classroom!</u> Try the Dino-mite Dinosaur Gingerbread cookie recipe included in this unit. What a wonderful way to bring closure to a very special unit of study. Remember, any of the recipes in this book can be sent home as a homework assignment or as a family learning activity. Children learn by doing so...let them bake and then eat cookies...dinosaur cookies, that is!!!

THE NEWS ABOUT DINOSAURS

by Patricia Lauber

First Edition   **Vol. #1**

Date:

Scientists once believed that _____

_____. The news about dinosaurs is _____

_____. by _____

Dazzling Dinosaur Reporter

Dinosaur Data Sheet

My Name: _____

Dinosaur's Name: _____

Tell About Your Dinosaur:

1. _____

2. _____

3. _____

4. _____

The most amazing fact that I learned about this dinosaur is _____

Draw a picture of your dinosaur.

Dino-mite Dinosaur Cookies

1/2 c. sugar
1/2 c. shortening
1/2 c. dark molasses
1/4 c. water
3/4 tsp. salt

3/4 tsp. ground ginger
1/2 tsp. baking soda
1/4 tsp. ground allspice
2 1/2 c. flour
raisins (for eyes)

Beat sugar, shortening, molasses and water in a large bowl at a low speed until blended. Beat one minute longer at medium speed. Stir in the remaining ingredients, except the raisins...those are for the dinosaur's eyes! Cover and refrigerate 1-2 hours. Heat oven to 375º. Sprinkle surface with flour and roll dough with a rolling pin to a 1/4 thickness. Cut out cookies with dinosaur cookie cutters and add raisins for eyes. Lift carefully with a spatula to an <u>ungreased</u> cookie sheet. Bake 8-10 minutes. Let cool a few minutes, then remove from the cookie sheet.

Dinolicious!

Dinosaur Masks

Tyrannosaurus Rex

Dinosaur Masks

CUT OUT

CUT OUT

Brachiosaurus

Dinosaur Masks

Diplodocus

Headbands for Dinosaur Script

Paleontologist #1

Paleontologist #2

Paleontologist #3

♥ **Note:** Simply reproduce the headbands and staple to sentence strips.

Reading Certificate

This award is presented to

_____

in honor of superior reading achievement.

Date _____

_____
Teacher's Signature

_____
Parent's Signature

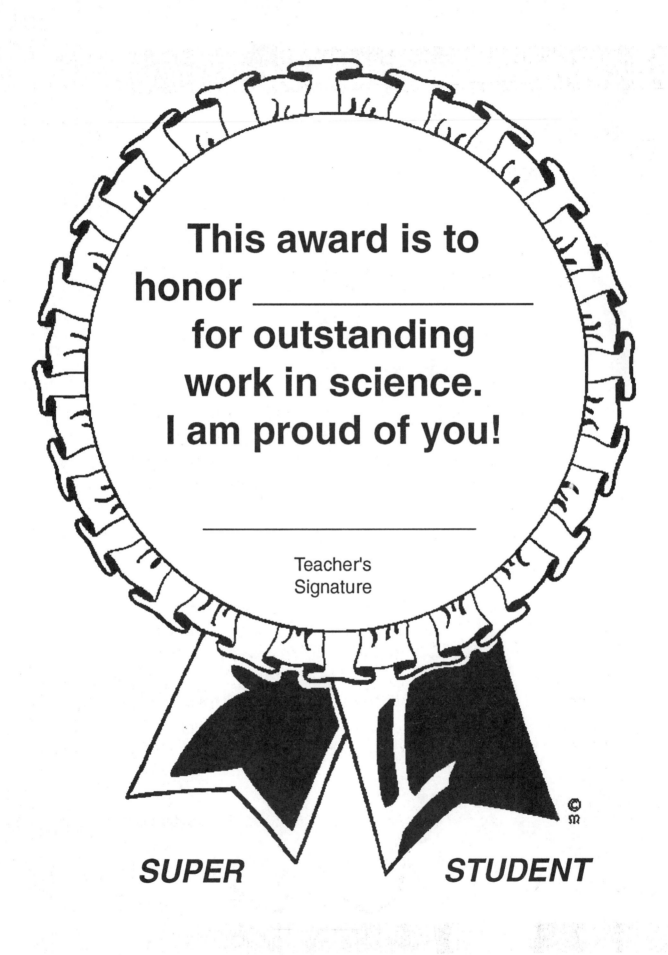

This award is to honor _____ for outstanding work in science. I am proud of you!

_____
Teacher's
Signature

SUPER   STUDENT